LITTLE Wise Guides

ALL ABOUT
BULLYING

Lesley Ely

Illustrated by Mike Phillips

Hodder
Children's
Books

a division of Hodder Headline Limited

To Cally, Jo and Adam

Text copyright 2001 © Lesley Ely
Illustrations copyright 2001 © Mike Phillips
Cover illustration copyright 2001 © Nick Sharratt

Published by Hodder Children's Books 2001

Design and typesetting by Michael Leaman

10 9 8 7 6 5 4 3 2 1

ISBN: 0 340 77901 2

Printed by The Guernsey Press Company Limited.

Hodder Children's Books
a division of Hodder Headline Limited
338 Euston Road
London NW1 3BH

Contents

Introduction

You may be reading this because you feel bullied. Or maybe your friend is being bullied. Either way, you want the bullying to stop.

You can stop bullying by understanding it. Knowing **why** people bully helps you stay safe. Understanding makes you powerful – it gives you confidence. Use your power – start building a bullying-free zone!

We shall start by looking carefully and asking questions. The grown-up word for this is **investigation**. The first thing to do with bullying is to **investigate.**

Keep an eye out for Henry the mouse throughout the book – you can spot him on several pages.

He is joined by his friends to help explain bullying.

I hope you enjoy reading this book – it should help you sort out your bullying problems!

Lesley Ely

You may be reading this book by yourself, or you may be reading it with your mum or dad. There are notes at the back for your parents to read – these start on page 61.

WHAT IS BULLYING?

Bullying isn't simple.

The trouble with bullying is everybody thinks
it's simple. Everybody asks "Who hit first?".
When they know who hit first, they think
they've found a **bully**. They call the person
who was hurt a **victim**. They think a
bully is one sort of person. They think a
victim is a different sort of person.

But, THAT'S WRONG. It's not that simple!

Bullying is a mix-up.

Bullying isn't simple, it's complex.
It's a tangle of different bits...

Complex things are like wool after a kitten has played with it.
Everything is in a muddle – the wool is tangled and knots have come from nowhere.

That's what bullying is.
It isn't neat balls of bully you can knit into something useful.
Bullying is a muddle.
Bullying is always a mix-up.

To sort it out we need to **investigate**.
Then we can make up our minds what to do.

Even grown-ups are sometimes bullied.

They may be bullied by people they work with.
They may be bullied at home.
They may even be bullied by people they have just met...

Grown-ups who bully each other
often bully children too.
**A person who bullies is often
being bullied by someone else.**

Some children even bully their mums
and dads. Bullying is always a big mix-up!

Bullying happens in a tangle of people.

Understanding bullying is hard when you're in a tangle, but it isn't impossible. It takes a cool head and cool thinking.

YOU CAN DO IT.
When you understand how it works,
you worry less.
When you are not too worried
you feel stronger inside.
Then you can deal with it.

Here's how it works.

Picture the people in your school.
Your school is a mixture of children and grown-ups:
pupils, teachers, the headteacher, the school secretary, dinner ladies, the caretaker, cleaners, governors.

We all feel safe and happy.

People tangles!

The lives of the people in school tangle together just like balls of wool in a bag. Each person affects the others.

The way each person feels affects the way the others feel. We are all different, but we all have the same feelings. We all need to feel safe. We are all scared of being lonely. We all need friends. That's the way it is for all of us.

Who's thinking what?

If we feel good about ourselves, we get on well with each other.

Some woolly ball people are neatly wound up.
They feel good about themselves.
They don't unravel easily.
They roll about happily.
They are all okay
– okay by themselves,
okay together.

I bounced highest.

So you did. Well done.

They fit in with each other like shapes in a wonderful pattern.

We are **ALL** like this some of the time.

Feeling bad
makes muddles.

Sadly, some woolly ball people are coming undone. They feel bad about themselves. When they are jumbled together they unravel easily.
They get in a muddle.
It's not their fault.
They can't help it.

We are **ALL** like this sometimes too.

Feeling bad causes bullying. Bullying makes us feel bad.

If nobody helps, things go wrong.
Pretty soon, everybody gets in the tangle.
Bullying happens.

What a tangle!

Bullying hurts everybody.

Even happy friendly people get dragged into bullying. People muddles are like that.

Nobody knows what to do.

I was happy until she hit me. Then I began to unravel.

I was happy until I saw what happened to you two. Now I'm scared it might happen to me.

I was happy until they called me names. Now I feel like I'm coming undone.

She doesn't like me. I can tell by her mean look.

What if that happens to me? I'd better look fierce, just in case!

A playground can be a lonely place if you feel scared.

Most schools are kind places.

If one of us begins to unravel, we all try to help. Grown-ups and children are kind to each other.

We help each other. We check each other out now and again.

We make sure everyone is okay.

Kind people won't bully. Kind people look after each other.

Falling out isn't always bullying.

Falling out isn't always bullying.
People fall out, they even fight. But it's not always bullying.
It might just be a disagreement.
It's not bullying when two people are evenly matched.
It's not bullying every time people are grumpy with each other.

Being bossy isn't bullying. Bossy boots may be kind and friendly. When we are fed up with the bossy stuff we just tell them.

Bullying isn't about being bossy or shy. Bullying IS about being unkind.

Bullying is making someone feel bad on purpose. It's bullying when someone deliberately tries to make us miserable. We are bullying when we know we are being mean and we don't stop.

It's bullying when we are deliberately unkind.

Bullying is about power.

Power isn't good OR bad.
It's just the way things are.
We all want power.
When we have power, we get what we want.

We all listen to some people more than others.
Those are often the people who have more power.

Big, strong people may have more **power**
than **little** people.
Grown-ups usually have more power than children.

A group may have more **power** than one
by himself.

We feel strong together.

I don't feel strong by myself.

Let's ask him to play with us.

That's a **GOOD** use of power!

18

Large groups may have more power than small groups.

Power comes in all sorts of ways.

Some people have more power than others because they are – clever, great at football, rich, popular and so on.

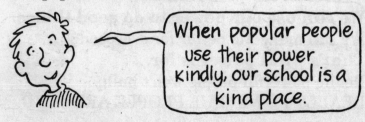

Truly powerful people want the best for us all.

We can use our power to help each other.

We can use our power to do good things.
We can make life better for everybody.
That's what power is for...
Really powerful people won't bully.
REALLY POWERFUL PEOPLE ARE KIND.

Misusing power is BULLYING.

Taking more than our fair share is **bullying**.

Trying to make other people feel bad is **bullying**.

You can't have any of this. I want it.

Popular people have power because everybody likes them.
They have a special responsibility. They can create happiness or cause misery.
Some people ALWAYS choose to be kind.
That's why everybody likes them.

Their power is confidence power.
Confidence power comes little by little.

It comes from the outside-in, and from the inside-out!

PATS AND ZAPS

Confidence power comes from PATS!

A **pat** can be a hug, a smile, or a friendly word. The grown-up word for pat is 'affirmation'. Pats make us feel big and strong inside. They give us **confidence power!**

We all know how to give pats – we were born good at it. We do it without knowing!
Once we know how **pats** work we can give them on purpose. Pats are full of energy! Pats multiply! Pats have the power to stop bullying!

These are 'outside – in' pats...

A smile is a great pat!

These are inside-out pats...

I can run!

I was kind!

I can skip!

I can read!

I can help!

I can swim!

I've got a friend!

I pat myself when I try and succeed!

Pats stop zaps!
Turn the page to find
out all about zaps.

Zaps are bad for us!

A **zap** is being ignored, belittled, or hurt. The grown-up word for zap is 'negation'. Zaps make us feel small. Zaps unravel us.

Sometimes we zap by mistake.
We feel sad when we see how bad our zap made someone feel.

Some of us get too many zaps.
Zaps make us unkind! Zaps make us bully!
Zaps sap our confidence.
Zaps make our power leak away.

Here's how zaps work...

People sometimes zap each other about stuff they can't help – their schoolwork, or the way they look.

DELIBERATE ZAPPING IS ALWAYS BULLYING!

The **worst** kind of bullying is saying bad things about a person's family, his skin colour, her religion, the clothes he wears or the way she talks.

I'm too busy to talk to you.

Get lost!

Stupid!

Can't you do anything?

You are rude!

You did that wrong.

Go away!

You are lazy!

You are selfish!

You are bad!

You are useless!

Being ignored is the biggest zap of all!

The more zaps we get the meaner we get!

Getting too many zaps makes even the kindest people lash out.

Some of us get so many zaps we even learn to zap ourselves.

BEN, JOE, TOM & BARRY

Let's investigate.

Can you spot the **pats** and **zaps** in the stories coming up?

One day at playtime, big Tom hit little Ben.
Ben's big brother Barry hit Tom back.
Tom cried.

Ben's friend Joe saw everything happen.
He was a **witness**.

It's not fair! Ben started it!

Tom hit little Ben, so I hit Tom! I think that's fair!

Tom is a big bully!

I'm a witness. I saw what really happened. Should I tell my teacher?

Being a witness.

Joe decides to tell the truth.
He tells what really happened.
He is a witness.

Joe's teacher, Mrs Jones, asks Joe some careful questions. Then she asks other children who saw what happened. She sends Tom, Ben and Barry to stand by the wall to think about what they did. All three boys miss their playtime. Mrs Jones says nobody behaved well!

Think what you might have done differently. Think how you could have made things better.

Now let's see what really happened.

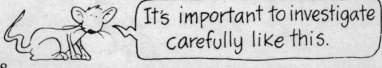

It's important to investigate carefully like this.

Zapping caused everything.

Ben called Tom names.
Ben said bad things about Tom's mum and dad.
He said Tom was a coward.
Tom got more and more upset.
He got so upset he lashed out and hit Ben.

You are stupid! You are useless! You let goals in! Can't you do anything?

You are right. I am stupid. But I'm still bigger than you!

Ben and Tom are both coming undone. Why is Ben so unkind?

Ben gets zapped at home. He's scared of his big brother Barry.
Zapping Tom makes Ben feel powerful.
Zapping Tom makes Ben feel better about the zapping HE gets from brother Barry.

This is how zapping spreads bullying. It's like an illness that everybody catches. When zapping starts, we don't know where it will end.

Being a witness is hard.

Joe's side of the story...

I feel awful. I don't know Tom that well and Ben is my best friend. Perhaps I can just keep quiet and not tell what I saw? Ben will never forgive me if I blab. He may even keep me out of the football game.

What do YOU think? What would YOU say to Joe?

You have to tell. It's the right thing to do.

Bullying will only stop if we ALL tell the truth.

If Ben can keep you out of football for telling the truth, he may be bullying you. How do you feel about that?

You can't let Tom take the blame. You know it was partly Ben's fault.

Talk to Ben. Tell him you want to be friends, but you WON'T join in with bullying. Explain that not telling the truth would be joining in.

30

Tom's side of the story...

Ben's popular. He's quick and clever and captain of football. He often teases me for being stupid and slow. He says he's joking, but it doesn't feel like a joke to me. I know it's not right to hit, but I'm not sorry I hit Ben. It serves him right. Everybody picks on me! This isn't my fault!

I'm not bullying - he is!

We always think OTHERS are bullying.
We never think WE are.

What would YOU say to Tom?

I think Ben was bullying you. Now everyone thinks YOU are bullying!

Come and play with me if it happens again.

When people call ME names, I say 'buzz off'. I don't get cross. They stop when they find they can't upset me.

Barry's side of the story...

I don't know Tom very well. I was mad with him because he hurt my brother. Tom was bullying, so I thought it was okay to hit him back. If I hit Ben at home my dad hits me. So I hit Tom when he hit Ben. Isn't that what you're supposed to do?

What would YOU say to Barry?

Bullying isn't right just because grown-ups do it. Everybody has to decide for themselves.

Maybe you bully because your dad bullies you. But you can choose for yourself - you don't have to follow your dad's bad example.

We are all responsible for our own actions.

You could say sorry to Tom.

Barry, Ben and Tom all acted the way they did because they were scared.

When people are scared their bodies make special energy to fight or run away!

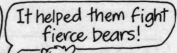

Long ago, this energy helped people escape from tigers!

It helped them fight fierce bears!

That's why, when we can't run away, we sometimes lash out! We get so scared, the part of our brain that acts without thinking just fights, as if other people are fierce bears! The fight button just switches itself on.

Sometimes we can tell ourselves that people aren't bears, but if we are **really** scared we **all** fight like wild creatures.

The best way to stop people lashing out is to make sure **nobody** ever feels so scared.

WHAT TO DO

If we don't help stop bullying, we are helping to keep it.

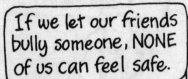

If we let our friends bully someone, NONE of us can feel safe.

If we let someone be bullied and don't help, we can never be sure that WE are safe.

What can I do? I'm scared to face the bullies.

We can tell our teachers and mums and dads, and keep on telling.

We can write to our head teacher if we are too scared to talk about it. Or we can write to the chairman of Governors of our school.

2, Willow Gardens
Tree Lane
Anytown

20th December 2001

Mr Balamb
Chairman of Governors
Woollyball School
Sheep Lane
Anytown

Dear Mr Balamb

Please will you help us. We are worried about our friend Paul. He is scared and unhappy because some people in our school call him names in the playground.

Please will you talk with our Headteacher about helping Paul and making our school a bullying-free zone. We would like our school to be a place where nobody has to feel scared.

Thank you for your help.

Yours sincerely

Joe and emma (class 3)

WHAT IF?

Sometimes we feel bullied when we misread each other's faces.

Humans are made to work together. We work better if we know a lot about each other. So we watch each other closely. We notice every little signal and decide what it means.

Being so clever can make life difficult for us. Humans are clever because we can picture things. (The grown-up word for this is 'imagination'.) We can picture anything at all.

A tiny red elephant with blue stripes? A huge yellow mouse bigger than a house?

We can easily picture things, even impossible things.

We can imagine problems we haven't got.

We can picture a 'what if' that isn't really there.
We picture the 'what if' that might happen next.

I heard a noise! What if there's a monster under my bed?

I see my friends talking. What if they are talking about me? What if they don't like me? What if they are planning to be mean to me? Ha! I'll get them before they get ME!

Pictures of 'what ifs' can make us just as cross and upset as real stuff.

Picturing problems we haven't got makes us accidentally **zap** ourselves. Then we feel so bad we **zap** other people. **Suddenly we are all zapping each other!** We feel bullied when we think other people are talking about us. When we investigate we often find misunderstandings.

SALLY, LIZ, JENNY & JAS

Let's investigate missing conversations!

This story often happens in school.
There is no hitting, only misunderstandings.
Feelings get hurt instead. It's just as painful.

Sally, would you mind looking after Liz until she settles in?

Course I will.

Sally, Jenny and Jas are good friends. Liz is new. Mrs Jones introduces Liz to Sally. Liz is quiet because she's new, but she's happy when the other girls ask her to join in at playtime. They are all kind girls.
What could go wrong?

You'd be surprised!

One day Sally's mum meets Liz's mum. She invites Liz and her mum to tea after school.

Come and have a cup of tea.

That would be great!
Our house is full of boxes.

Liz and Sally play together. Liz is fun to play with and not at all quiet now.
At school the next day, Liz makes Sally giggle.

So far so good!

That's what YOU think!

Jenny accidently zaps herself!

Jenny feels jealous when Liz makes Sally laugh. Jenny likes making people laugh herself. She especially likes making Sally laugh because Sally has an infectious laugh. It makes others join in, even if they haven't heard the joke!

Everybody works hard that morning in school and nobody talks much. This means that Sally can't explain the joke. She catches Jenny's eye and whispers: "Tell you later". But she doesn't. When playtime comes, she forgets all about it.

Sally has accidentally zapped Jenny.
Jenny has accidentally zapped herself.

A misunderstanding turns into a muddle.

Jenny is really fed up and goes off in a huff.
Liz and Sally don't notice because they are too
busy laughing.
Jas does notice and goes after Jenny. Jas is
kind and asks Jenny what is wrong.
Jenny sulks and won't say. Jas tries to cheer
her up, but Jenny won't smile.

When we are part of a group we feel safe. It is
easy to picture how lonely we would feel outside the group. It scares us! We feel as bad as
we would if we were really left out and lonely!

41

The muddle gets worse.

A bit later, Sally and Liz look for Jenny and Jas. They see Jenny and Jas talking.

Sally pictures Jenny and Jas talking about her.
"Those two are boring!" she says.
Liz is confused. She wants to be friends with everybody. She doesn't know what to say.
She wants to say: 'Let's go and ask them what's the matter.'
But she doesn't, because she doesn't want to risk upsetting Sally.

Liz wants to help, but she doesn't know how.

Next day, there is a bad feeling in class.
All the girls feel upset.
Each girl sees something different.

Sally is upset because she thinks Jenny and Jas don't like her.

Jenny is upset because she thinks she has lost her best friend Sally.

Jas is upset because she hasn't a clue what's going on, and nobody seems to want to tell her.

Liz is upset because she wants to be friends with everybody, and now she feels she has to choose.

Missing conversations can make us ill.

This is a people tangle.
Everybody feels lost and everybody is afraid of being left out.

The girls are scared to say how they feel.
They don't mean this to happen.
They are all trying to do their best.
They don't know how to get things right again.

I wish one of the girls would say 'Hey, what's going on? I want to be friends!' Human talk must be powerful! Even things people DON'T say can make them unhappy.

Not talking to each other can make us ill.

One day, Jas is ill with a tummy upset. She isn't at school and Jenny feels lonely without her.

At playtime Jenny stays behind to talk to her teacher. She says she has a sore tummy too.

Liz and Sally are upset about the bad feeling, so they decide to wait for her. She takes so long they think she doesn't want to be friends. So they go off to the school's garden.

When Jenny comes back at last she can't find them anywhere. She is very, very sad.

They could have waited. They knew I had no one to play with. They must hate me.

Jenny is zapping herself again.

That evening, Jenny's mum sees Jenny's sad face.

"What's the matter?" she asks Jenny.
"Nobody played with me at school today", Jenny tells her. "And my throat hurts", she weeps.

Her mum listens carefully. She has lots of questions.

Jenny's mum wonders if Jenny is being bullied. She feels sad for Jenny.
She doesn't want to interfere. She knows Jenny has to sort the friendship out herself, but she decides Jenny's teacher will want to know.
She hopes a **conversation** will help.

Jenny's mum goes to see Mrs Jones.

I haven't seen anything that looks like bullying, but I'll check it out.
I'll have a chat with the girls.

Thanks for listening. I feel better for this chat. I'll be able to help Jenny now.

We need **investigation** to check what happened.
We need **imagination** to picture ourselves in the other person's shoes.
Most of all, we need a **conversation**!

Better be careful with imagination. Picturing 'what ifs' started this whole muddle!

You're dead right!

Mind-reading and chat power!

We can all read each other's minds.
We pick up clues like the look on someone's face, or the way a person behaves.
We imagine how it would feel to BE that person. (We call this 'putting ourselves in someone else's shoes'!)
Then we make a guess about how the person feels. Mind-reading is a great skill.

Mind-reading can make us kinder to each other. It helps us work well together.

BUT... mind-reading can't do everything.

We may THINK we know how the other person feels. But sometimes we get it wrong.

Mind-reading isn't enough! We need to TELL each other how we feel. We need to chat!

48

Good mind-readers still need to talk!

49

Chat power!

Chat helps us get problems out in the open.
This makes them easier to sort out.
Chat helps us ALL feel good!
Chats stop problems starting!
Chats pat!

Mrs Jones called Sally, Liz, Jenny and Jas in for a chat. They talked for a long time. It was a good conversation.

I was upset because I thought Jenny and Jas were talking about me. Jenny used to be my best friend.

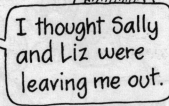

I thought Sally and Liz were leaving me out.

I felt lonely because I was new. I wanted to be friends with everyone. Sally was upset, so I tried to be kind. Sally was my only friend, I didn't want to lose her.

Chats about how we feel really help.

I wanted everyone to be friends. I was sorry for Jenny because she was upset. I tried to be kind to her. I didn't understand why she fell out with Liz and Sally.

That's because **I didn't fall out !**

You needed this chat weeks ago! You are good friends. You just had a **Misunderstanding.** Let's talk about why you became friends in the first place.

Pats make friends.

The girls put **pats** into the **chat!** Every pat makes someone feel better.

I like Sally because she used to laugh at my jokes.

I miss your jokes. They were so funny!

I like Sally because she was kind to me when I was new.

I like Sally because she listens. She makes me feel fun to be with.

I like Jenny because she's been my friend since nursery school.

I like Jenny because she makes me laugh.

I like Jenny because she's clever and she has a nice face!

Pats in chats make us feel good!

I like Jas because she's easy-going and helps people.

I like Jas because she's nice to everybody.

I like Jas because she's kind. She helps when someone is upset.

I like Liz because she's a good laugh when she's not being shy!

I like Liz because she's quiet, but she remembers what you say!

I like Liz because she thinks I've got a nice face. I think she's got a nice face too!

Now it's all sorted, we can see how this muddle happened!

Liz changed things for the others by joining the group. She couldn't help it and neither could they.

Change can be hard, but we are all good at it. When things change we need time to get used to it.

We have to change to fit in with the changes!

When our world **changes** we change **what** we do AND the **way** we do things. Even making a new friend changes our world a tiny bit.

STOPPING BULLYING

Each person's world is different.

If we are happy we notice good things. We don't notice much bad stuff.

My world is what I see. It's the way I think about it.

Mine too!

It's the same the other way round.
When we feel bad, we don't notice good things.

When we feel good about ourselves, our world is a good place.

When I like myself, I like other people too.

When we feel bad, the good things are invisible!

We don't notice someone wanting to be friends with us.

You can't play with us!

I'd love to play but she doesn't see me!

We don't notice someone who needs our help.

Nobody will play with me!

Nobody will play with me!

We don't notice things that would help us feel good. We only see zaps and bullies!

We need a zap shield!

A zap shield makes us bully proof!

Zap shields are made of all the pats we get and give ourselves!

Pats stop zaps!

Every time we get a pat our zap shield gets stronger! We can start by giving pats to ourselves!

When we feel good about ourselves nobody upsets us for long.

Every time I do something I enjoy I add a pat to my zap shield!

I love to skip!

I add a pat to my zap shield when I do something active! Swimming, running, football... anything!

Why people bully.

People bully when they feel very, very unhappy.
They bully to feel better about other people
bullying them. Someone else is bullying the
person bullying you (even though you can't see it).

People who bully us are ALWAYS scared.

- They may be scared nobody likes them.

- They may be scared of changes in their lives.

- They may be scared of being alone.

- They may be scared that we are getting the
  attention they need – they may be jealous.

- They may be scared that if they don't act big
  and angry, someone may **bully THEM.**

- They may be scared of people we don't
  know about.

THAT'S WHY WE ALL HAVE TO HELP!

When we become pat people, our world feels like a kind place.

When we give pats, we find nice people.
When we give pats, nice people find us!

We can ALL make people feel good if we choose to.

We can choose to PAT, not zap. Pats and chats stop zaps!

Bullying-free zones are possible!

We have the power – let's use it!

GLOSSARY

Affirmation
Affirmations are what we do or say to make ourselves and other people feel good. In this book they are called 'pats'.

Conversation
Conversation is talking with each other. Conversation is having a chat. Conversations help us get on with each other. We can tell each other how we feel and find out how to help each other. Conversations stop us getting the wrong ideas about each other. Conversations with grown-ups help us deal with bullying. Conversations with our friends help us deal with bullying too.

Imagination
Imagination is being able to picture things in our minds. We are clever enough to picture what other people might be thinking or feeling. Being able to imagine how other people feel helps us understand them. We have to be careful with imagination. We can make mistakes. We are sometimes too good at picturing things we are scared might happen. When we are scared we sometimes imagine things that make us fall out or be cross with each other.

Investigation
Investigation is looking into things to find out what really happened and why. When we think bullying is going on we need to ask questions and have conversations. That way we can understand and decide how to help each other. That way we don't make things worse by mistake.

Negation
Negations are what we do or say to make ourselves and other people feel bad. In this book they are called 'zaps'.

NOTE FOR PARENTS

This book is for 7 to 9 year olds worried by bullying in school. It explains why bullying happens and how to deal with it.

Children develop socially by adapting to the needs of others. Teachers set boundaries which support harmony and self-esteem. But teachers aren't all seeing and they can't be everywhere. From an early age, girls and boys instinctively try to control each other. They are caring but know how to wind each other up. They recognise their power to exclude and will use it. That's what humans do.

A healthy social identity grows from self-esteem. The playground is a great place to develop this, but it isn't always easy. It takes practice. Like the grown-up world, the playground doesn't always run smoothly. People fall out. They may get their own way by anti-social means. They may be anxious, stressed or downright angry. Big labels such as BULLY and VICTIM are applied to unhappy boys and girls who don't want to be either. Labels make self-esteem, kindness and harmony harder to achieve.

Children are born with social sensitivity. It makes them powerful and vulnerable at the same time. Some children are naturally confident, some are timid. All have the right to be safe from bullying. Even children have a duty to help others enjoy the same right. Understanding how the social world works helps them find a positive place in it. Just like we did.

Bullying-free zones are possible.

SORTING BULLYING OUT

A 10-point plan for parents

1 Make sure your child understands that nobody has the right to bully.

2 Be clear about what bullying is.
Bullying is deliberate physical or emotional intimidation. The adult (legal) world may call it assault, slander, racial harassment, discrimination, theft etc. Bullying (including hitting, spiteful whispering, name calling, exclusion and taking someone else's possessions) is just as unacceptable in our playgrounds as it is in the adult world.

3 Recognise that ALL children take part in bullying sometimes.
Passive participants (or onlookers) are involved even though they don't want to be. They are often the most confused. They need help sorting out the difference between 'telling tales' and responsible reporting.

4 Don't label any child 'bully' or 'victim'.
These are negative terms which make BOTH children feel bad about themselves. We can talk about bullying without labelling individuals.

5 Investigate if you suspect bullying.
Common signs of fear are: bedwetting, tearfulness, uncharacteristic aggression toward younger siblings, tantrums, sleeplessness, weakening of the immune system (increased susceptibility to common ailments).

6 Take your child's fear seriously.

Social skills are complex, important and not easy to acquire. Problems matter.

7 Be positive and optimistic.

Expect success. Whether your child is bullying or being bullied, the situation is usually temporary. Most of the time children resolve things themselves with a bit of help. Talk with the teacher and headteacher. It is their job to make school a safe place. They will help all they can.

8 Focus on your child.

Talking helps. Listen with your full attention.

9 Help your child increase his self-esteem.

Confident children with high self-esteem are more able to cope with social difficulties. Find ways to give 'pats'. Show that you can solve disagreements amicably in your own relationships. Be there.

10 Help the vulnerable child.

Children who meet constant negation ('zaps') are more likely to bully and be bullied. ANY child is vulnerable to bullying and being bullied when overwhelmed by pressures. Family events like death, divorce, illness, moving house or school, even a new baby, can all make a child more susceptible. Children having difficulty with basic reading and writing skills often feel 'left out' and distressed. If you think this is a problem, don't delay. Get help.

FINDING OUT MORE

Childline
Tel: 0800 1111
(keep trying if the lines are busy)

Or write to: Freepost 1111, London N1 0BR
(no postage stamp needed)

Or try the **Childline** website:
www.Childline.org.uk

Kidscape
Tel: 0207 730 3300
Kidscape has leaflets and books about bullying.

ABOUT THE AUTHOR

Lesley Ely is a former primary headteacher with
a special interest in Personal and Social Education.
Her experience includes working with children and
parents affected by some of the traumas of childhood
(divorce, bullying etc). Lesley believes that learning to
talk, think about and understand feelings will help all
children. The ideas in this book arise from 30 years
of her conversations with children...who always knew
much more than they thought they did.